COMIC-STRIP MATH: MINI-STORY PROBLEMS

40 Reproducible Cartoons With Dozens of Story Problems That Build Essential Math Skills and Tickle Kids' Funny Bones!

by Dan Greenberg

SCHOLASTIC
PROFESSIONAL BOOKS

New York • Toronto • London • Auckland • Sydney

Cover and interior design by Grafica Inc.
Cover and interior illustrations by Jared Lee.

ISBN 0-439-04383-2

Printed in the U.S.A.

TABLE OF CONTENTS

TABLE OF CONTENTS

INTRODUCTION

Following on the heels of *Comic-Strip Math,* this book boldly goes where few books have gone before—across the frontier that separates serious mathematics from mirth, merriment, and good fun. *Comic-Strip Math: Mini-Story Problems* features story problems that are both great stories and great problems at the same time.

The book contains 40 new cartoons, organized into six sections that cover a wide array of critical math skills, including whole-number problems, fractions, decimals, mental math, money, measurement, and more. The lessons in this book will help you meet the National Council of Teachers of Mathematics curriculum standards.

USING THIS BOOK

Comic-Strip Math: Mini-Story Problems can supplement your core mathematical program in many ways: as part of an interdisciplinary program that integrates reading and math, or as an in-class reward for work well done. You may also use this book to introduce new problem-solving skills to students who are ahead of the class, or to review topics for students who need extra help.

Each cartoon encourages students to apply their visual, verbal, spatial, and reasoning skills to interpret situations and solve mathematical problems.

Lessons accompanying the cartoons start out with easy-to-solve problems and gradually progress to more difficult problems. Lessons culminate with a Super Challenge problem that invites students to apply what they've learned in a new or unique way.

While individual lessons focus on a specific math topic, problems are by no means limited to that topic. A lesson on division, for example, will contain mostly division problems. But it may also require students to use other computational skills such as multiplication, addition, and subtraction, as well as basic problem solving, critical thinking, and reasoning skills.

FINALLY . . .

The purpose of this book is to help students see math as a fun and interesting part of their real world. But don't stop there. Encourage students to look for other ways to incorporate math and mathematical thinking into their own lives. Show students that the more math they learn, the more fun it becomes!

Name: _____

THE TREE starring Rowena Pig and Itchy Squirrel

FIGURE IT OUT!

1. The apple that hit Rowena Pig fell from a branch that is 30 feet above the ground. How far is the branch from the top of the 100-foot tree?

_____

2. Rowena's ladder reaches up to 50 feet. How many feet shorter is the ladder than the 100-foot tree?

_____

3. Starting on the ground, Itchy Squirrel climbs 20 feet up the tree. Then she stops to rest. She climbs 37 feet more and stops to rest again. How many feet did Itchy climb up the tree?

_____

4. Rowena climbs 47 feet up the tree. Then an apple falls on her. The apple fell from a branch that is 92 feet up the tree. How many feet did the apple drop before hitting Rowena?

_____

5. Itchy climbs 57 feet up the 100-foot tree. Then she climbs down 28 feet. How many feet is she from the top of the tree?

_____

SUPER CHALLENGE: Itchy is 20 feet from the top of the 100-foot tree. She jumps straight across to a second tree. Now she's 30 feet from the top of the second tree. How tall is the second tree?

Name: _____

WHO'S GOT THE BUTTON? starring Molly Mouse and Ant Betty

They say that every 3 seconds, somebody somewhere loses a button.

Good gracious!

You'd think that person would learn to keep track of his buttons after a while.

FIGURE IT OUT!

1. If a button is lost every 3 seconds, how many buttons are lost in 60 seconds?

_____

2. Ant Betty finds some buttons. She gives 7 buttons to each of her 8 nieces. How many buttons did she find?

_____

3. Molly Mouse organizes 6 groups of mice to look for lost buttons. Each group has 5 mice. How many mice are there in all?

_____

4. One group of mice finds many buttons and they put them into 9 bags. Each bag contains 14 buttons. How many buttons did the mice find?

_____

5. A second group of mice collects 20 bags containing a total of 160 buttons. Each bag contains the same number of buttons. How many buttons are in each bag?

_____

SUPER CHALLENGE: Suppose 20 mice want to form teams with an equal number of mice on each team. How many different-size teams can they form?

7

Name: _____

A FAMILIAR FACE starring Monica Bear and Squirmy Worm

Do you know how to get to Worm University?

I sure do! A lot of my brothers and sisters go to Worm University.

Really! Say, you look familiar. Where have I seen your face before?

Gee, I don't know. Maybe . . .

. . . on the front of my head?

FIGURE IT OUT!

1. Squirmy Worm has 100 brothers. Forty of them are students at Worm University. How many brothers are <u>not</u> students at Worm U?

_____

2. Twenty of Squirmy's brothers will graduate from Worm University. Squirmy plans to give each brother 4 pebbles as gifts. How many pebbles does he need in all?

_____

3. Some of Squirmy's sisters will also graduate from Worm U. He plans to give them twigs as gifts. Squirmy has 150 twigs. Each sister will get 5 twigs. How many sisters will graduate?

_____

4. Two worms gave speeches at the Worm University graduation. One speech lasted 68 minutes. The other speech was 13 minutes longer. How many minutes was the second speech?

_____

5. A total of 1,056 worms will graduate from Worm U. Of those, 356 plan to become soil farmers and 119 plan to work in the sanitation business. The rest plan to become lawyers. How many worms plan to be lawyers?

SUPER CHALLENGE: Do more or less than half of the graduating class in problem 5 want to become lawyers?

Name: _____

PAIN IN THE NECK starring Dr. Woovis the Dog and Rowena Pig

FIGURE IT OUT!

1. Dr. Woovis wants Rowena Pig to take 2 red pills a day for 10 days. How many red pills will Rowena take in all?

_____

2. Red pills come in two different-size bottles. The large bottle contains 100 pills. The small bottle contains 40 pills. Which has more pills—one large bottle or 3 small bottles?

_____

3. Harry Horse needs to take 6 blue pills a day. If a bottle of blue pills has 84 pills, how many days will it last?

_____

4. How many days will a bottle of 294 blue pills last if a patient takes 6 blue pills per day?

_____

5. Rudy Rabbit needs to take 9 green pills a day for 2 weeks. How many green pills will he take in all?

_____

SUPER CHALLENGE: Dr. Woovis wants Squirmy Worm to take 8 purple pills a day for 3 weeks, then 6 purple pills a day for the following 2 weeks. How many purple pills will Squirmy take in all?

Name: _____

HOOP DREAMS starring Molly Mouse, Rudy Rabbit, and Judy Frog

FIGURE IT OUT!

1. If Michael Jordan can jump 3 feet off the ground and Judy Frog can jump 2 times as high wearing her basketball sneakers, how high can Judy jump?

_____

2. Wearing her new Super Springy sneakers, Judy can jump 3 times as high as with her regular basketball sneakers. How high can Judy jump with her new sneakers?

_____

3. In 6 games, Judy scored 17, 13, 21, 16, 9, and 20 points. How many points did she score in all?

_____

4. Judy's team played 9 games. The team scored 50 points in each game. How many points did the team score in all the games?

_____

5. Judy scored 30 points in the championship game. She scored three 3-point baskets and five 1-point baskets. How many 2-point baskets did she score?

_____

SUPER CHALLENGE: In the championship game, Judy scored the highest with 30 points, which is 6 more than the second-highest scorer. The second-highest scorer scored 6 more points than the third-highest scorer, and so on for all five players on the team. How many points did the team score in all?

THE SQUIRM-ULATOR starring Squirmy Worm and Moovis the Cow

FIGURE IT OUT!

1. Help out Squirmy Worm. What do you get when you multiply 6 by 7, then subtract 13? Use a calculator to check the answer.

_____

2. Squirmy multiplies 8 by 5, then divides the product by 4. What is the answer?

_____

3. Moovis the Cow multiplies 11 by 14. Then she divides the product by 7. What is the answer?

_____

4. Multiply the number of days there are in a week by 12. Subtract 24. What is the answer?

_____

5. How old are you? Multiply your age in years by 17. Then add or subtract to get a total of 200. What number did you add or subtract?

_____

SUPER CHALLENGE: On which day of the month were you born? Multiply this number by 3. Is the product higher than 100?

Name: _____

WHITE SOCKS, BLACK SOCKS starring Rowena Pig and Judy Frog

FIGURE IT OUT!

1. Rowena Pig is wearing 1 white sock and 1 black sock. What fraction of the socks she's wearing is white? What fraction is black?

_____

2. Rowena puts 7 socks in the washing machine. Four of them are black and 3 are white. What fraction of the socks is black? What fraction is white?

_____

3. Rowena hangs 8 socks out to dry. Two of the socks are black and 6 are white. What fraction is black? Write your answer in simplest form.

_____

4. Judy Frog brings 6 socks on a trip. One third of the socks are red. The rest are green. How many socks are red? How many are green?

_____

5. Six out of 10 socks are blue. The rest are red. What fraction of the socks is red? Write your answer in simplest form.

_____

SUPER CHALLENGE: Judy has 12 socks. One third of them are white. One fourth of them are red. The rest are yellow. How many socks are yellow? How many socks are white and red?

Name: _____

FRIENDSHIP starring Ed and Fred, the Singing Giraffe Brothers

FIGURE IT OUT!

1. Ant Betty is Ed's good friend. To talk to Ed, she has to climb up his 12-foot-long neck. Betty climbs 3 feet up Ed's neck. What fraction is 3 of 12? Write the fraction in simplest form.

_____

2. Ant Betty climbs 6 feet up Ed's 12-foot neck. What fraction is 6 of 12? Write the fraction in simplest form.

_____

3. What fraction of Ed's 12-foot neck did Betty climb after going 8 feet? Write the fraction in simplest form.

_____

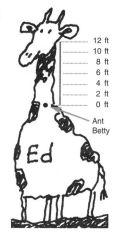

4. How many feet must Ant Betty climb to cover $\frac{3}{4}$ of Ed's 12-foot neck?

_____

5. Ant Betty climbs $\frac{5}{6}$ of the way up Ed's neck. How many more feet does she need to go to reach the top of his neck?

_____

SUPER CHALLENGE: Fred has a 14-foot neck. How many feet would you have to climb to get halfway up Fred's neck? How many feet would you have to climb to get halfway up Ed's neck? Which distance is greater? How much greater?

Name: _____

AT THE MOVIES starring Woovis the Dog and Judy Frog

FIGURE IT OUT!

1. Mint gum runs out of flavor after $7\frac{3}{5}$ minutes. Suppose Woovis the Dog can make gum flavor last $3\frac{1}{5}$ minutes longer. How long will the gum's flavor last?

_____

2. Woovis eats one jelly bean in $1\frac{2}{3}$ minutes. He eats a milk ball in $1\frac{1}{6}$ minutes. How long does it take him to eat the jelly bean and milk ball?

_____

3. A lollipop lasts 12 minutes. After $6\frac{1}{2}$ minutes, how many more minutes will the pop last?

_____

4. Woovis sees two movie previews. One lasts $6\frac{3}{4}$ minutes and the other lasts $4\frac{5}{8}$ minutes. How long do both previews last?

_____

5. Judy Frog comes in $12\frac{1}{2}$ minutes late to *Revenge of the Flies* and stays until the end. The movie runs for 70 minutes. How much of the movie does she see?

_____

SUPER CHALLENGE: Woovis starts eating his popcorn when *Frogs, Dogs, and Choo-Choo Trains* begins. The movie runs for $72\frac{1}{4}$ minutes. Woovis's popcorn lasts for $48\frac{1}{2}$ minutes. How many minutes of the movie will be left when Woovis finishes his popcorn?

Name: _____

MIDNIGHT IN THE BARN starring Molly Mouse and Harry Horse

FIGURE IT OUT!

1. There are 24 horse stalls in the barn. One half of the stalls had horses in them when Molly Mouse came running by last night. How many stalls had horses?

_____

2. Each of 18 horses eats $\frac{2}{3}$ of a bale of hay. How many bales do 18 horses eat?

_____

3. Each cow eats $\frac{2}{5}$ bale of hay every morning. How many bales do 10 cows eat?

_____

4. Half of the chickens in the barn laid an egg. Half of those eggs were white. What fraction of all the chickens laid a white egg?

_____

5. Four sevenths of the pigs eat at a trough. Two sevenths of the pigs roll in the mud. There are 28 pigs. How many pigs eat in the trough and roll in the mud?

_____

SUPER CHALLENGE: There are 50 horses in the corral. Three fifths of the horses wear saddles. Half of the horses wearing saddles have a rider. What fraction of all the horses in the corral has a rider?

Name: _____

BEACH DAY starring Woovis the Dog and Monica Bear

FIGURE IT OUT!

1. Woovis the Dog drives Monica Bear $\frac{3}{5}$ of a mile to the beach. A cab ride costs 50¢ per mile. How much did the ride cost?

_____

2. At the beach, Woovis picks up a chicken. He drives $\frac{3}{5}$ of a mile down Shore Road. Then he turns right on Coop Street and drives $\frac{2}{5}$ of a mile to a hen house. How far did he drive in all? How much did the ride cost?

_____

3. Woovis drives a skunk $\frac{9}{10}$ of a mile to a skunk den. Then he drives a cat $\frac{4}{5}$ of a mile to a milk bar. Which animal did Woovis drive farther? How much farther?

_____

4. Woovis drives $\frac{3}{8}$ of a mile to the park. Then he drives $\frac{1}{2}$ of a mile to the zoo. How far does he drive in all?

_____

5. The Surf Hotel, Beach Hotel, and Walt's Drive-In are all on the same road. Surf Hotel and Beach Hotel are 1 mile apart. Walt's Drive-In is between the two hotels. It is $\frac{3}{10}$ of a mile from Beach Hotel. How far is the drive-in from Surf Hotel?

_____

SUPER CHALLENGE: Woovis drives $\frac{5}{9}$ of a mile to Beach Hotel. Then he drives $\frac{1}{6}$ of a mile to the beach. How far does he drive in all?

16

Name: _____

HAT HOLE starring Moovis the Cow and Harry Horse

FIGURE IT OUT!

1. Harry Horse's hat measures $14\frac{5}{8}$ inches around. Woovis the Dog's hat measures $6\frac{3}{8}$ inches around. How much larger is Harry's hat?

_____

2. Woovis puts 2 snowballs into Harry's hat. Each snowball weighs $3\frac{2}{3}$ ounces. How much do the 2 snowballs weigh?

_____

3. Harry splits a 9-ounce snowball into 4 equal-size pieces. How much does each piece weigh?

_____

4. Moovis the Cow splits an $8\frac{1}{3}$-ounce snowball into 5 equal-size pieces. How much does each piece weigh?

_____

5. Compare the pieces in problems 3 and 4. Which pieces weigh more? How much more do they weigh?

_____

SUPER CHALLENGE: Suppose you fill a hat with 20 ounces of lemonade. Then you pour the lemonade evenly into either 5 blue cups or 6 red cups. Which would have more lemonade—a blue cup or a red cup?

Name: _____

DUET starring Ed and Fred, the Singing Giraffe Brothers

FIGURE IT OUT!

1. Ed and Fred are the Singing Giraffe Brothers. Ed is 24.2 feet tall. Fred is 26.5 feet tall. How much taller is Fred?

_____

2. Fred stands next to a 30-foot tree. How many feet taller is the tree than Fred?

_____

3. Ed stands on a 6.3-foot platform. The platform is next to a 30-foot tree. How much higher is Ed than the tree?

_____

4. Fred is standing on the same 6.3-foot platform. How much higher is Fred than the 30-foot-tall tree?

_____

5. Jed is the third of the Singing Giraffe Brothers. He is only 18.6 feet tall. Jed wears elevator boots to make himself as tall as Ed. How high are Jed's elevator boots?

_____

SUPER CHALLENGE: Ed, Fred, and Jed want to wear elevator boots so they can all be the same height. If they all want to appear to be 32 feet in height, how tall should each pair of boots be?

Name: _____

THE LADDER starring Judy Frog and Chuck Mantis

FIGURE IT OUT!

1. Judy Frog climbs up 3 steps of the ladder. If each step is 0.4 meters apart, how high is Judy off the ground?

_____

2. Judy climbs up 16 steps of the ladder. How many meters off the ground is she?

_____

3. Chuck Mantis climbs the ladder to a height of 8 meters. If each step has a height of 0.4 meters, how many steps does he climb?

_____

4. Judy climbs 50 steps up the ladder. How many meters does she climb?

_____

5. Which is higher—60 steps of the ladder or 25 meters? How much higher?

_____

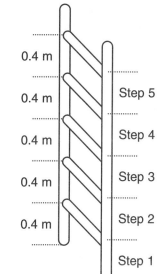

0.4 m

0.4 m .... Step 5

0.4 m .... Step 4

0.4 m .... Step 3

0.4 m .... Step 2

Step 1

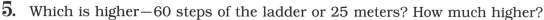

SUPER CHALLENGE: A ladder is 100 meters high. Each step is 0.4 meters apart. How many steps does the ladder have?

Name: _____

THE PICNIC starring Rowena Pig and Squirmy Worm

Doggone it! I wish we had brought the TV with us on this picnic.

Why?

'Cause that's where I left the picnic basket. On top of the TV!

FIGURE IT OUT!

1. The picnic basket weighs 11.4 pounds. The TV weighs 20 pounds. How much more does the TV weigh?

_____

2. The picnic basket will hold 8 pounds of food. How many 0.8-pound sandwiches will it hold?

_____

3. Which weighs more—a 0.8-pound tuna sandwich or a 0.26-pound cheese sandwich? How much more?

_____

4. Suppose Rowena Pig makes lunch bags that include a 0.8-pound sandwich and a 0.18-pound pickle. How much will each lunch bag weigh? Rowena makes 9 lunch bags. What is the total weight of all the lunches?

_____

5. There are 3 kinds of lunch boxes. The first weighs 1.6 pounds. The second weighs 2.2 pounds. The third weighs 2.5 pounds. Rowena wants to bring 3 lunch boxes that weigh exactly 6 pounds. Which combination of lunch boxes should she bring?

_____

SUPER CHALLENGE: Using the lunch boxes in problem 5, find three more ways to fill the picnic basket with 3 lunch boxes without going over the 6-pound limit.

Name: _____

THE GREAT ESCAPE starring Woovis the Dog and Rowena Pig

FIGURE IT OUT!

1. Woovis the Dog can escape from a bolt lock in 0.75 minutes. It takes him 0.4 minutes longer to escape from a key lock. How long does it take Woovis to escape from a key lock?

_____

2. It takes Woovis 1.8 minutes to escape from a combination lock. How long will it take him to escape from 3 combination locks in a row?

_____

Woovis's Escape Times
Combination Lock: 1.8 minutes
Bolt Lock: 0.75 minutes
Key Lock: _____ minutes

3. How long will it take Woovis to escape from 1 bolt lock, 3 key locks, and 4 combination locks?

_____

4. In the Underwater Trick, Woovis can hold his breath underwater for 6 minutes. How many bolt locks can he unlock in this time?

_____

5. How many key locks can Woovis unlock in 9.2 minutes?

_____

SUPER CHALLENGE: How many bolt locks can Woovis unlock in exactly 24 minutes?

Name: _____

WRESTLE-MANIA starring Monica Bear and Rudy Rabbit

FIGURE IT OUT!

1. At the weigh-in, Monica Bear weighs 452.2 pounds. Rudy Rabbit weighs in at 3.8 pounds. How much more does Monica weigh?

_____

2. If Rudy weighs 3.8 pounds, how many pounds would he need to gain to wrestle in the heavyweight division of 275 pounds or more?

_____

3. How many pounds heavier is Monica than the minimum weight for the heavy-weight division?

_____

4. Woovis the Dog weighs 41.8 pounds. How many times heavier is Woovis than Rudy?

_____

5. How many times heavier is Monica than Rudy?

_____

SUPER CHALLENGE: Does Monica weigh more than 10 times as much as Woovis? About how many times heavier is Monica than Woovis?

Name: _____

FUNNY MONEY starring Rudy Rabbit & Woovis the Dog

FIGURE IT OUT!

1. Rudy Rabbit has two $10 bills. How much money does he have?

_____

Use mental math to solve each problem.

2. What is the value of four $10 bills? Six $10 bills? Ten $10 bills?

_____

3. What is the value of eight $100 bills? Sixteen $100 bills? Twenty-five $100 bills?

_____

4. Rudy has $400. How many $100 bills equal $400? How many $10 bills equal $400?

_____

5. Rudy has $5,700. How many $100 bills could he get for $5,700? How many $10 bills could he get for $5,700?

_____

SUPER CHALLENGE: Fill in the chart by multiplying. What pattern do you see?

1 x 20	2 x 20	3 x 20	4 x 20	5 x 20
20				

6 x 20	7 x 20	8 x 20	9 x 20	10 x 20

Name: _____

MASTERPIECE starring Moovis the Cow and Squirmy Worm

FIGURE IT OUT!

1. Moovis the Cow sells her paintings for $9.95 each. How many paintings could Squirmy Worm buy for $20? Use estimation to find the answer.

_____

Use estimation to solve each problem.

2. How many $9.95 paintings could Squirmy buy for $50? For $80?

_____

3. Moovis sells her Deluxe paintings for $10.95 each. How many paintings could Squirmy buy for $100?

_____

4. Moovis has a new series of paintings called "Three Cows Sleeping in a Totally Dark Barn." Each painting sells for $6.02. Could someone buy 4 of these paintings with $20? Why or why not?

_____

5. How many $10 bills would Squirmy need to buy 3 paintings for $9.95?

_____

SUPER CHALLENGE: Woovis bought 10 paintings for $99.90. How much does each painting cost?

Name: _____

FOOD TO GO starring Woovis the Dog and Molly Mouse

FIGURE IT OUT!

1. Woovis the Dog found a $5 bill. Which item can he buy from the menu that will give the least change?

_____

DOGGIE DINER BREAKFAST SHOP

MENU

Kibble $1.79
Mouse Crumbs $1.39
Table Scraps $2.49
Crumbs & Cheese $3.19
Deluxe Scraps $3.79

2. Molly Mouse gets Crumbs & Cheese for breakfast. She pays with the $5 bill. With the leftover money, what can Woovis buy to eat?

_____

3. Which item can Woovis buy with the $5 bill that will give the <u>most</u> change?

_____

4. Which two items can Woovis buy with the $5 bill so that he gets about $1 back in change?

_____

5. Woovis ordered two items from the menu and gave the cashier the $5 bill. But the two items cost more than $6.50. Which two items did Woovis order?

_____

SUPER CHALLENGE: Can Woovis use the $5 bill to buy three <u>different</u> items from the menu? Why or why not?

Name: _____

MAKIN' CHANGE starring Squirmy Worm and Judy Frog

FIGURE IT OUT!

1. If Squirmy Worm has one quarter, how many more quarters does he need to get one dollar?

_____

2. Squirmy has dimes and nickels that add up to 50¢. He has 6 coins in all. What coins does he have?

_____

3. Judy Frog has $1 in quarters and dimes. She has 5 dimes. How many quarters does she have?

_____

4. Woovis the Dog has $1 in quarters and nickels. He has 1 quarter. How many nickels does he have?

_____

5. Judy has pennies, nickels, and dimes that add up to $1. She has 5 nickels and 3 dimes. How many pennies does she have?

_____

SUPER CHALLENGE: Squirmy has quarters, dimes, and nickels that add up to $1.60. He has 4 dimes and 9 nickels. How many quarters does he have?

Name: _____

THE WISE OLD PHILOSOPHER starring Woovis the Dog and Molly Mouse

> PRICES
> Truth .... 10¢
> Wise thoughts..... 12¢
> Flashes of insight.. 15¢
> Doughnuts....... 18¢
>
> *The Philosopher →*
>
> What would you like to know, my child?

> 10¢
> 12¢
> 15¢
> 18¢
>
> Tell me, oh wise one, what is at the end of everything?

> ...10¢
> ...12¢
> ...15¢
> ...18¢
>
> That's simple, my child. At the end of every-thing is the letter G.
>
> Sheesh!

FIGURE IT OUT!

1. Molly Mouse gives the Philosopher one dollar. How many 10¢ truths can she get for $1?

_____

2. Rudy Rabbit buys 2 truths, 2 wise thoughts, and 2 flashes of insight. How much does he spend?

_____

3. Moovis the Cow buys 2 truths, 2 wise thoughts, 2 flashes of insight, and 1 doughnut. She pays $1. How much change does she get back?

_____

4. Molly buys 4 truths, 6 wise thoughts, and 2 flashes of insight. How much does she spend?

_____

5. Rowena Pig spends exactly $1 on truth and doughnuts. She buys 1 truth. How many doughnuts does she buy?

_____

SUPER CHALLENGE: Think of one way to spend exactly one dollar on truths, wise thoughts, and doughnuts.

Name: _____

TAKE IT TO THE BANK starring Judy Frog and Chuck Mantis

FIGURE IT OUT!

1. A guppy saves $10 each month and puts it in the bank. How much money does she have in the bank after 6 months?

_____

2. A trout has $80 in his checking account. He takes out $16 to buy a large bag of fish food. Then he deposits $64 the following week. How much money does he have in his account?

_____

3. A sea horse has $200 in her checking account. She deposits $35. Then she takes out $150 to buy a saddle the following week. How much money is left in her account?

_____

4. Chuck Mantis wants to put $270 in the bank. If he saves $9 a week, how many weeks will it take him to reach $270?

_____

5. The bank will give Judy Frog a free insect catcher if she puts $500 in the bank. She has $486. But she needs to spend $40 of that money to fix her lily pad. How much more money will she need to get the insect catcher?

_____

SUPER CHALLENGE: A codfish put $15 in the bank in January. Each month after that, she deposits twice as much as she did the month before. How many months will it take her to save more than $200?

28

LIVE AT THE HA-HA COMEDY CLUB starring Woovis the Dog

FIGURE IT OUT!

1. Woovis the Dog's Thursday comedy show sells 38 tickets for $4.00 each. How much money does the sale of the tickets bring in?

_____

2. Woovis's Friday show sells 46 tickets for $4.75 each. How much money does the show take in?

_____

3. On Saturday morning, tickets cost $4.25. The Saturday morning show sells 50 tickets. How much money does the show take in?

_____

4. On Saturday afternoon, both $4.00 and $4.50 tickets are sold. In all, 22 tickets are sold for $4.00, and 28 tickets are sold for $4.50. How much money does the show take in?

_____

5. Which show took in more money—the Saturday morning show or the Saturday afternoon show? How much more?

_____

SUPER CHALLENGE: The Saturday night show has tickets for $4.50 and $5. Forty tickets for $4.50 are sold. In all, the show takes in a total of $300. How many $5 tickets are sold?

Name: _____

NEW JEANS starring Rowena Pig and Woovis the Dog

FIGURE IT OUT!

1. All jeans are on sale for $\frac{1}{4}$ off the regular price of $28. How much is $\frac{1}{4}$ of $28?

_____

2. How much would Rowena Pig pay for a pair of jeans on sale?

_____

3. Rowena wants to buy 2 pairs of jeans on sale. How much will she pay?

_____

4. In the Bonus Sale, you pay regular price for the first pair of jeans, then get $\frac{1}{2}$ off each additional pair. The regular price is $28. How much will Rowena pay for 2 pairs of jeans?

_____

5. Suppose Rowena decides to buy 3 pairs of jeans. How much will it cost to buy them for the sale price of $\frac{1}{4}$ off? How much will it cost to buy the 3 pairs using the Bonus Sale? Which sale would you choose?

_____

SUPER CHALLENGE:

The chart compares the regular, Sale, and Bonus Sale prices. Complete the chart.

	Regular Price	Sale Price	Bonus Sale Price
1 pair	$28		
2 pairs	$56		
3 pairs			
4 pairs			
5 pairs			

Name: _____

NICE HAT starring Woovis the Dog and Rudy Rabbit

FIGURE IT OUT!

1. Rudy Rabbit decides he couldn't wait 1,000 years to call. Instead, he would wait only 17 years. To the nearest ten, how many years does Rudy wait? _____

2. Suppose Rudy calls after 54 years. To the nearest ten, how many years is this?

_____

3. Suppose Rudy waits 133 years. To the nearest ten, how many years is this? To the nearest hundred?

_____

4. Suppose Rudy waits 452 years. To the nearest hundred, how many years is this? To the nearest ten?

_____

5. Suppose Rudy calls after 687 years. To the nearest hundred, how many years is this? To the nearest thousand?

_____

SUPER CHALLENGE: Rounded to the nearest hundred, a number equals 1,000. What is the smallest value that this number can have?

Name: _____

GOT THE TIME? starring Rudy Rabbit and Harry Horse

FIGURE IT OUT!

1. The time on Harry Horse's first watch reads 11:30. What time is it on the second watch?

_____

2. Suppose Harry's first watch is 1 hour ahead of the second watch. The second watch reads 8:00. What time is it on Harry's first watch?

_____

3. The time on a clock is 5:08. What time will it be in 17 minutes? What time will it be in 45 minutes?

_____

4. The time on a clock is 11:30. What time will it be in 35 minutes? What time will it be in 1 hour and 15 minutes?

_____

5. The time on a clock is 2:37. What time will it be in 4 hours and 14 minutes? What time will it be in 9 hours and 23 minutes?

_____

SUPER CHALLENGE: The time on a clock is 3:22. What time was it 24 minutes earlier? What time was it 56 minutes earlier?

Name: _____

THE MOLLY MOUSE SHOW starring Molly Mouse and Woovis the Dog

FIGURE IT OUT!

1. At 12 noon, the alarm on a clock is set to go off in 30 minutes. Where will the hands of the clock be when the alarm goes off? What number will be covered? _____

2. At 12:00, the minute hand and the hour hand line up at exactly the same place on a clock. The alarm is set to go off the next time the two hands line up in exactly the same place. What time will it be when the alarm goes off?

_____

3. An alarm is set to ring every 30 minutes starting at 2:00. When will it ring between 2:00 and 4:30?

_____

4. An alarm is set to ring every hour and a half beginning at 11:00. Will the alarm ring at 2:30 or 3:30?

_____

5. An alarm rings every 12 minutes starting at 12:00. When will it ring between 12:00 and 2:00?

_____

SUPER CHALLENGE: An alarm is set to ring every 20 minutes starting at 12:00. How many times will the alarm ring from 12:00 and 7:00?

Name: _____

KEEPING COOL starring Chuck Mantis and Squirmy Worm

What's gray, has a cool job, and stops working after 31 days?

I don't know. What?

An air conditioner with a 30-day guarantee.

FIGURE IT OUT!

1. Chuck Mantis buys an air conditioner on January 1. The air conditioner has a 30-day guarantee. On what day will the guarantee expire?

_____

2. Squirmy Worm goes grocery shopping every 3rd day. If he shops on January 11, what are the next two dates he will go shopping again?

_____

3. Chuck shops every 6th day. If he shops on a Saturday, on what day of the week will he go shopping next?

_____

4. Woovis the Dog goes shopping on January 20. He goes shopping 12 days later. On what date does he go shopping again?

_____

5. How many days are there from January 15 to February 12?

_____

SUPER CHALLENGE: Rowena Pig goes grocery shopping every 3rd day. If she shops on Saturday, January 1, on what date will she shop on a Saturday again?

Name: _____

STOP SIGN starring Rowena Pig and Woovis the Dog

There were two stop signs back there. You didn't stop for the first one.

STOP

HIGHWAY PATROL

You're right! But you still shouldn't write me a ticket.

Why not?

S

Because I stopped TWICE for the second stop sign.

Oh.

FIGURE IT OUT!

1. Rowena Pig rides 25 yards on her bike to get from the first stop sign to the second one. How many feet apart are the stop signs? (One yard equals 3 feet.) _____

2. At the second stop sign, Rowena skids to a quick stop. Her bike leaves a 7-foot skid mark in the sand. How many inches long is the skid mark?

_____

| **Measurements** |
| 1 foot = 12 inches |
| 1 yard = 3 feet |
| 1 mile = 5,280 feet |

3. Rowena rides 4 miles across town. How many feet does she ride?

_____

4. Rowena rides 30 feet. How many inches does she ride?

_____

5. Rowena rides 99 yards. How many feet does she ride?

_____

SUPER CHALLENGE: Rowena rides 40 yards. How many inches are there in 40 yards?

Name: _____

TRASH TALK starring Moovis the Cow and Molly Mouse

FIGURE IT OUT!

1. Moovis the Cow carries a 3-pound bag of garbage to the dump. One pound equals 16 ounces. How many ounces does the bag weigh?

_____

2. How many ounces are there in a 9-pound bag of garbage? A 22-pound bag of garbage?

_____

| **Measurements** |
| 1 pound = 16 ounces |
| 1 foot = 12 inches |

3. A bag weighs 64 ounces. How many pounds does it weigh?

_____

4. How many inches are there in a 14-foot-high pile of trash?

_____

5. How many feet are there in a 480-inch-high pile of trash?

_____

SUPER CHALLENGE: Measure the length of your classroom in feet. How long is your classroom in inches?

Name: _____

HIGHWAY ROBBERY starring Officer Woovis the Dog and Rowena Pig

FIGURE IT OUT!

1. Rowena Pig lives on the corner of 2nd Street and Avenue A. From her house she rides up Avenue A to 4th Street. How many blocks does she ride?

_____

2. Rowena rides from the bank on 2nd Street and Avenue D to the bike shop on 5th Street and Avenue D. How many blocks does she ride?

_____

3. Rowena rides up Avenue A from her house to the park on 5th Street and Avenue E. How many blocks does she ride?

_____

4. Rowena rides up 4th Street from Avenue B to Avenue E. Then she turns around and rides back to Avenue A. How many blocks does she ride?

_____

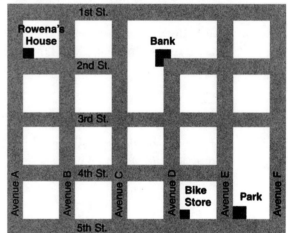

5. Rowena goes for a bike ride. She starts at 3rd Street and Avenue E. She rides to 3rd Street and Avenue B. Then she turns right to 2nd Street and Avenue B. How many blocks does she ride?

_____

SUPER CHALLENGE: Rowena can go from her house to the bank by riding up 1st Street or by riding up 3rd street. Which way is shorter?

Name: _____

THE HAMMER starring Woovis the Dog and Rudy Rabbit

FIGURE IT OUT!

1. Rudy Rabbit pounds 3 nails into a piece of wood. The nails are *not* in a straight line. What shape will he get if he draws lines to connect the nails?

_____

2. Rudy pounds 4 nails to form 4 right angles. The nails are all 3 inches apart. What shape does Rudy make? Draw the shape.

_____

3. Woovis the Dog attaches a pencil to a nail with a string. Then he pulls the string tight and swings it around. What shape does the pencil draw?

_____

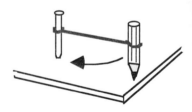

4. Moovis the Cow pounds 4 nails to form 4 right angles. Two nails are 3 inches apart. Two other nails are 4 inches apart. What shape does Moovis make? Draw the shape.

_____

5. Each side of a triangle is 10 inches long. What is the distance around the triangle?

_____

SUPER CHALLENGE: Here are some true statements about a square: It has 4 sides. It has right angles. Write one other true statement about a square.

Name: _____

A BEAR IN FULL starring Monica Bear and Ant Betty

FIGURE IT OUT!

1. Monica Bear's new mirror measures 72 inches by 60 inches. What is the perimeter of the mirror? (Perimeter is the distance all the way around.) _____

2. Another mirror is shaped like a square. That means that all 4 sides are the same length. The mirror's perimeter is 24 inches. How long is each side?

_____

3. Ant Betty's full-length mirror is $3\frac{1}{2}$ inches across and $4\frac{1}{2}$ inches down. What is its perimeter?

_____

4. Which has a greater perimeter, a mirror that measures $8\frac{1}{2}$ inches across and 12 inches down or a mirror that measures $12\frac{1}{2}$ inches across and 8 inches down?

_____

5. Mirror A measures 5 inches across and 7 inches down. Mirror B measures 8 inches across and 3 inches down. Which mirror's perimeter is bigger? How much bigger?

_____

SUPER CHALLENGE: A mirror is shaped like a rectangle. Its width is twice as long as its height. The mirror is 11 inches high. What is its width? What is the mirror's perimeter?

Name: _____

LUCKY SEVEN starring Rudy Rabbit and Monica Bear

FIGURE IT OUT!

1. What number is missing from this number pattern?

5, 11, 17, 23, 29, ___, 41, 47

_____

2. The underlined number in this pattern is wrong. What number should go in its place? 4, 12, 20, 28, 36, <u>42</u>, 52

_____

3. Replace the underlined number in this pattern with the correct number.
2, 4, 8, 16, <u>24</u>, 64, 128

_____

4. Write the next three letters in this pattern: A, C, E, G, I, __, __, __.

_____

5. Write the next three numbers in this pattern: 407, 396, 385, 374, 363, __, __, __.

_____

SUPER CHALLENGE: Find the wrong number in this pattern. Then write the number that should go in its place. 1, 3, 9, 27, 36, 243

Name: _____

ROOF ROOF starring Woovis the Dog, Chuck Mantis, and Judy Frog

And he said, ROOF! ROOF!

Woovis Live! at Ha - Ha Comedy Club.

I never get these ROOF jokes.

Neither do I.

They seem to go right over my head.

I know what you mean.

FIGURE IT OUT!

1. Section A (below) at Ha Ha's has 3 rows with 3 seats in each row. In how many seats would you have a neighbor on both your left side and your right side? _____

2. In how many seats in Section A would you have a neighbor on only one side?

_____

Section A

3. Section B has 3 rows with 4 seats in each row. In how many seats would you have a neighbor on both your left side and your right side?

_____

Section B

4. In how many seats in Section A would you have a neighbor on all 4 sides—on your left, on your right, in front of you, and behind you?

_____

5. In how many seats in Section B would you have a neighbor on all 4 sides?

_____

Section C

SUPER CHALLENGE: Section C has 3 rows with 5 seats in each row. In how many seats in Section C would you have a neighbor on all 4 sides? In how many seats would you have a neighbor on both your left side and your right side?

Name: _____

MAGIC SHOW starring Woovis the Dog and Ant Betty

> **FIGURE IT OUT!**
>
> **1.** Woovis smashed several pump-
> kins. The graph below shows the
> results. How many pieces did the 10-
> pound pumpkin smash into?
>
> _____

2. How many pieces did the 30-pound pumpkin smash
into?

_____

3. How many more pieces did the 40-pound pumpkin
smash into than the 30-pound pumpkin?

_____

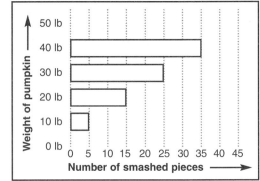

4. How many 10-pound pumpkins do you need to
smash to get the same number of pieces in a 40-pound smashed pumpkin?

_____

5. Look at the pattern on the graph. How many pieces would you expect a 50-pound
pumpkin to smash into? Draw a bar on the graph.

_____

SUPER CHALLENGE: How many pieces would you expect a 100-pound pumpkin
to smash into?

Name: _____

WEATHERMAN starring Woovis the Dog and Rudy Rabbit

FIGURE IT OUT!

1. Showers on Monday morning produced 0.5 inches of rain by noon. By 6 p.m., a total of 2 inches of rain had fallen. How many inches of rain fell between noon and 6 p.m.? _____

2. On Tuesday, 1.2 inches of rain fell. Two more inches of rain fell the next day. How many inches of rain fell on Wednesday?

_____

3. The graph shows the high temperatures for Wednesday through Sunday. On which day was the highest temperature reached? The lowest? What was the difference between the two temperatures?

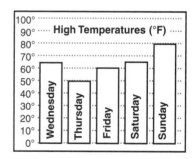

_____

4. Between which two days did the temperature drop 15 degrees? Increase by 15 degrees?

_____

5. Saturday's low temperature was 38°. How many degrees did the temperature rise to reach Saturday's high temperature?

_____

SUPER CHALLENGE: What was the average high temperature for all five days shown on the graph?

43

Name: _____

TALENTED TONGUE starring Harry Horse and Judy Frog

I'm one of the world's smartest horses.

Prove it.

I can speak 5 different languages.

Let's hear them.

OK, here goes. Bow-wow! Meow! Cluck cluck! Ribbit! And, oh yeah. Moo!

Wow, I'm impressed!

FIGURE IT OUT!

1. Using RIBBIT and CROAK, a frog can make these 2-word phrases: RIBBIT-CROAK and CROAK-RIBBIT. What 2-word phrases can a dog make of BARK and RUFF? (Use each word only once in each phrase.) _____

2. How many different 2-word phrases can a dog make out of the words BARK and GRR? Write each arrangement.

_____

3. How many different 2-word phrases can a dog make out of the words BARK, GRR, and RUFF? Write each arrangement.

_____

4. How many different 2-word phrases can a cat make out of the words MEOW, PURR, and SSS? Write each arrangement.

_____

5. How many different 3-word phrases can a cat make out of the words MEOW, PURR, and SSS? Write each arrangement.

_____

SUPER CHALLENGE: How many different 3-word phrases could a cat make out of the words MEOW, PURR, and SSS if each phrase must start with the word PURR?

Name: _____

MATH WHIZ starring Squirmy Worm, Ant Betty, and Itchy Squirrel

Squirrels are good at math.

How so?

Watch this. Hey, Itchy Squirrel. What's 17 take away 17?

That's correct. 17 take away 17 is NOTHING!

She said nothing.

FIGURE IT OUT!

1. Itchy Squirrel scores 86, 73, 47, 93, and 81 on her math tests. What is her high score? What is her low score?

_____

2. The range of Itchy's scores is the difference between her high and low scores. What is her range?

_____

3. Arrange Itchy's scores in problem 1 from lowest to highest. The median is the middle score in the group. What is her median score?

_____

4. The mean score is the average score. To find the mean, add all the scores. Then divide the total by the number of scores. What is the mean of Itchy's scores in problem 1?

_____

5. The mode is the score that appears the most in a group. Find the mode from this group of quiz scores: 16, 15, 18, 20, 15, 13, 15, 13, 19.

_____

SUPER CHALLENGE: Roll a number cube 25 times. Record the scores. Find the range, mean, median, and mode of your scores.

ANSWERS

THE TREE
(p. 6)

1. 70 feet
2. 50 feet
3. 57 feet
4. 45 feet
5. 71 feet
Super Challenge: 110 feet

WHO'S GOT THE BUTTON?
(p. 7)

1. 20 buttons
2. 56 buttons
3. 30 mice
4. 126 buttons
5. 8 buttons
Super Challenge: 6 teams

A FAMILIAR FACE
(p. 8)

1. 60 brothers
2. 80 pebbles
3. 30 sisters
4. 81 minutes
5. 581 worms
Super Challenge: More than half want to become lawyers.

PAIN IN THE NECK
(p. 9)

1. 20 pills
2. 3 small bottles
3. 14 days
4. 49 days
5. 126 pills
Super Challenge: 252 pills

HOOP DREAMS
(p. 10)

1. 6 feet
2. 18 feet
3. 96 points
4. 450 points
5. 8 two-point baskets
Super Challenge: 90 points

THE SQUIRM-ULATOR
(p. 11)

1. 29
2. 10
3. 22
4. 60
5. Answers will vary.
Super Challenge: Answers will vary, but none of the products should be higher than 100.

WHITE SOCKS, BLACK SOCKS
(p. 12)

1. $\frac{1}{2}$ white, $\frac{1}{2}$ black
2. $\frac{4}{7}$ black, $\frac{3}{7}$ white
3. $\frac{1}{4}$ black
4. 2 red socks, 4 green socks
5. $\frac{2}{5}$ red
Super Challenge: 5 yellow socks, 7 red and white socks

FRIENDSHIP
(p. 13)

1. $\frac{1}{4}$
2. $\frac{1}{2}$
3. $\frac{2}{3}$
4. 9 feet
5. 2 feet
Super Challenge: You would need to climb 7 feet to get halfway up Fred's neck. To get halfway up Ed's neck, you would need to climb 6 feet. The distance halfway up Fred's neck is greater than the distance halfway up Ed's neck by 1 foot.

AT THE MOVIES
(p. 14)

1. $10\frac{4}{5}$ minutes
2. $2\frac{5}{6}$ minutes
3. $5\frac{1}{2}$ minutes
4. $11\frac{3}{8}$ minutes
5. $57\frac{1}{2}$ minutes
Super Challenge: $23\frac{3}{4}$ minutes

MIDNIGHT IN THE BARN
(p. 15)

1. 12 stalls
2. 12 bales
3. 4 bales
4. $\frac{1}{4}$ of the chickens
5. 24 pigs
Super Challenge: $\frac{3}{10}$ of the horses

BEACH DAY
(p. 16)

1. 30¢
2. 1 mile; 50¢
3. Woovis drove the skunk $\frac{1}{10}$ of a mile farther.
4. $\frac{7}{8}$ of a mile
5. $\frac{7}{10}$ of a mile
Super Challenge: $\frac{13}{18}$ of a mile

HAT HOLE
(p. 17)

1. $8\frac{1}{4}$ inches
2. $7\frac{1}{3}$ ounces
3. $2\frac{1}{4}$ ounces
4. $1\frac{2}{3}$ ounces
5. The $2\frac{1}{4}$-ounce snowballs weigh more. They weigh $\frac{7}{12}$ of an ounce more.
Super Challenge: blue cup

DUET
(p. 18)

1. 2.3 feet
2. 3.5 feet
3. 0.5 foot
4. 2.8 feet
5. 5.6 feet high
Super Challenge: Ed's boots should be 7.8 feet tall. Fred's boots should be 5.5 feet tall. Jed's boots should be 13.4 feet tall.

THE LADDER
(p. 19)

1. 1.2 meters
2. 6.4 meters
3. 20 steps
4. 20 meters
5. 25 meters is higher by 1 meter
Super Challenge: 250 steps

THE PICNIC
(p. 20)

1. 8.6 pounds
2. 10 sandwiches
3. The 0.8-pound tuna sandwich weighs 0.54 pounds more.
4. Each lunch bag will weigh 0.98 pounds. The total weight of the lunch bags is 8.82 pounds.

5. Two 2.2-pound lunches and one 1.6-pound lunch

Super Challenge: Three 1.6-pound lunches (4.8 pounds); two 1.6-pound lunches and one 2.5-pound lunch (5.7 pounds); two 1.6-pound lunches and one 2.2-pound lunch (5.4 pounds)

THE GREAT ESCAPE
(p. 21)

1. 1.15 minutes
2. 5.4 minutes
3. 11.4 minutes
4. 8 bolt locks
5. 8 key locks
Super Challenge: 32 bolt locks

WRESTLE-MANIA
(p. 22)

1. 448.4 pounds
2. 271.2 pounds
3. 177.2 pounds
4. 11 times heavier
5. 119 times heavier
Super Challenge: Yes. Monica weighs about 10.8 times more than Woovis.

FUNNY MONEY
(p. 23)

1. $20
2. $40; $60; $100
3. $800; $1,600; $2,500
4. 4 $100 bills; 40 $10 bills
5. 57 $100 bills; 570 $10 bills
Super Challenge:

1 x 20	2 x 20	3 x 20	4 x 20	5 x 20
20	40	60	80	100

6 x 20	7 x 20	8 x 20	9 x 20	10 x 20
120	140	160	180	200

Each answer is 20 greater than the previous answer.

MASTERPIECE
(p. 24)

1. 2 paintings
2. 5 paintings for $50; 8 paintings for $80
3. 9 paintings
4. No. Four paintings cost more than $24.
5. 3 $10 bills
Super Challenge: $9.99

FOOD TO GO
(p. 25)

1. Deluxe Scraps
2. Kibble or Mouse Crumbs
3. Mouse Crumbs
4. Table Scraps and Mouse Crumbs
5. Crumbs & Cheese and Deluxe Scraps
Super Challenge: Woovis can't buy three items with $5. The cheapest three items cost a combined $5.67.

MAKIN' CHANGE
(p. 26)

1. 3 quarters
2. 4 dimes and 2 nickels
3. 2 quarters
4. 15 nickels
5. 45 pennies
Super Challenge: 3 quarters

THE WISE OLD PHILOSOPHER
(p. 27)

1. 10 truths
2. 74¢
3. 8¢
4. $1.42
5. 5 donuts
Super Challenge: 7 truths, 1 wise thought, 1 donut OR 1 truth, 3 wise thoughts, 3 donuts OR 4 truths, 2 wise thoughts, 2 donuts

TAKE IT TO THE BANK
(p. 28)

1. $60
2. $128
3. $85
4. 30 weeks
5. $54
Super Challenge: 4 months

LIVE AT THE HA-HA COMEDY CLUB
(p. 29)

1. $152
2. $218.50
3. $212.50
4. $214
5. The Saturday afternoon show took in $1.50 more.
Super Challenge: 24 $5 tickets were sold.

NEW JEANS
(p. 30)

1. $7
2. $21
3. $42
4. $42
5. It costs $63 to buy 3 pairs of jeans at the sale price of $\frac{1}{4}$ off. With the Bonus Sale, it costs $56 to buy 3 pairs of jeans. The Bonus Sale is a better deal.
Super Challenge:

	Regular Price	Sale Price	Bonus Sale Price
1 pair	$28	$21	$28
2 pairs	$56	$42	$42
3 pairs	$84	$63	$56
4 pairs	$112	$84	$70
5 pairs	$140	$105	$84

NICE HAT
(p. 31)

1. 20 years
2. 50 years
3. 130 years; 100 years
4. 500 years; 450 years
5. 700 years; 1,000 years
Super Challenge: 950

GOT THE TIME?
(p. 32)

1. 11:45
2. 9:00
3. 5:25; 5:53
4. 12:05; 12:45
5. 6:51; 12:00
Super Challenge: 2:58; 2:26

THE MOLLY MOUSE SHOW
(p. 33)

1. The hour hand will be at 12 and the minute hand at 6; 6 will be covered.
2. 1:05
3. 2:00, 2:30, 3:00, 3:30, 4:00, 4:30
4. 3:30
5. 12:00, 12:12, 12:24, 12:36, 12:48, 1:00, 1:12, 1:24, 1:36, 1:48, 2:00
Super Challenge: 22 times

KEEPING COOL
(p. 34)

1. January 31
2. January 14 and January 17
3. Friday
4. February 1
5. 28 days
Super Challenge: January 22

STOP SIGN
(p. 35)

1. 75 feet
2. 84 inches
3. 21,120 feet
4. 360 inches
5. 297 feet
Super Challenge: 1,440 inches

TRASH TALK
(p. 36)

1. 48 ounces
2. 144 ounces in a 9-pound bag; 352 ounces in a 22-pound bag
3. 4 pounds
4. 168 inches
5. 40 feet
Super Challenge: Answers will vary.

HIGHWAY ROBBERY
(p. 37)

1. 2 blocks
2. 3 blocks
3. 7 blocks
4. 7 blocks
5. 4 blocks
Super Challenge: Riding up 3rd Street

THE HAMMER
(p. 38)

1. A triangle
2. A square
3. A circle
4. A rectangle
5. 30 inches
Super Challenge: Answers will vary, but could include: All sides of a square are the same length. The perimeter is always 4 times the length of one side.

A BEAR IN FULL
(p. 39)

1. 264 inches
2. 6 inches
3. 16 inches
4. Both mirrors have the same perimeter.
5. Mirror A has a bigger perimeter than Mirror B by 2 inches.
Super Challenge: The mirror's width is 22 inches, and its perimeter is 66 inches.

LUCKY SEVEN
(p. 40)

1. 35
2. 44
3. 32
4. K, M, O
5. 352, 341, 330
Super Challenge: The wrong number is 36. The number that should replace it is 81.

ROOF ROOF
(p. 41)

1. 3 seats
2. 6 seats
3. 6 seats
4. 1 seat
5. 2 seats
Super Challenge: 3 seats; 9 seats

MAGIC SHOW
(p. 42)

1. 5 pieces
2. 25 pieces
3. 10 pieces
4. 7 smashed pumpkins
5. 45 pieces
Super Challenge: 95 pieces

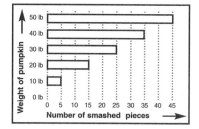

WEATHERMAN
(p. 43)

1. 1.5 inches
2. 3.2 inches
3. The highest temperature was reached on Sunday. The lowest temperature was reached on Thursday. The difference between the two temperatures was 30 degrees.
4. The temperature dropped 15 degrees between Wednesday and Thursday. The temperature increased by 15 degrees between Saturday and Sunday.
5. 27 degrees
Super Challenge: 64 degrees

TALENTED TONGUE
(p. 44)

1. BARK-RUFF, RUFF-BARK
2. You can make 2 phrases: BARK-GRR, GRR-BARK
3. You can make 6 phrases: BARK-GRR, GRR-BARK, BARK-RUFF, RUFF-BARK, GRR-RUFF, RUFF-GRR
4. You can make 6 phrases: MEOW-PURR, MEOW-SSS, PURR-SSS, PURR-MEOW, SSS-PURR, SSS-MEOW
5. You can make 6 phrases: MEOW-PURR-SSS, MEOW-SSS-PURR, PURR-MEOW-SSS, PURR-SSS-MEOW, SSS-PURR-MEOW, SSS-MEOW-PURR
Super Challenge: You can make 2 phrases: PURR-MEOW-SSS, PURR-SSS-MEOW

MATH WHIZ
(p. 45)

1. The high score is 93. The low score is 47.
2. The range is 46.
3. 47, 73, 81, 86, 93; median score is 81.
4. 76
5. 15
Super Challenge: Answers will vary.